The Garden and the Image of Truth

Retold by the Rose ... the One Who Always Believed

the Rose

Illustrated by the Lily

WestBow Press books may be ordered through booksellers or by contacting:

WestBow Press
A Division of Thomas Nelson & Zondervan
1663 Liberty Drive
Bloomington, IN 47403
www.westbowpress.com
1 (866) 928-1240

Art Credit to The Child within

ISBN: 978-1-5127-6127-6 (sc)
ISBN: 978-1-5127-6128-3 (e)

Library of Congress Control Number: 2016917798

Print information available on the last page.

WestBow Press rev. date: 11/15/2016

WESTBOW
PRESS®
A DIVISION OF THOMAS NELSON
& ZONDERVAN

Author's Note

This story is a much-condensed but nevertheless a truthful retelling of the many centuries-old tale of the Garden. It is not for the spiritually illiterate but for the child within.

"Except you become as little children and seek Truth you shall not enter the Garden and Kingdom of Light."

Chapter 1:

Truth

Before the dawning of the first day, there was Truth and Truth was with the Creator; Truth was Light. At that time, the earth was covered with water and darkness was upon the face of the deep. The Creator separated the earth from the water. Bang! The earth had a form.

Chapter 2:

Life and the Image of Truth

Next the Creator planted a Garden. It was a delightful Garden and full of life. It was a place where Truth could abide. The Garden would need a gardener so the Creator made a special lifeform. The gardener was formed after the Creator in the image of Truth and was called Life.

Chapter 3:

Jealous

Deceit was jealous of the Garden and the gardener. The Creator spoke to Life and said, "Life, you may eat freely of the fruit in the Garden but do not eat of the Tree of Knowledge of Light and Darkness. If you make the choice to partake of the Kingdom of Darkness, you will lose your rights to the Garden.

Chapter 4:

The Call to Life

Summer arrived, and the Garden had grown quite lovely. The Creator often walked with Life in the Garden in the cool of day. One day the Creator called to Life, and Life did not answer. "Life, where are you? What have you done?" And Life answered, "I have listened to Deceit, and I did eat."

Chapter 5:

Lost Rights

Autumn came clothed in glory. The wind gently shook the leaves from the trees. But the Garden was no longer the same. Life had been deceived, and instead of calling out to the Creator and confessing the error, Life had chosen to hide. Then Life made an excuse and tried to place blame. Truth went missing, and Life lost the rights to the Garden.

Chapter 6:

Hidden from View

Winter was approaching, and the Creator was lonely. Spring would be coming again, and without Life there would be no one to take care of the Garden. The error must be corrected. So, on a cold, wintry night, beneath a crescent moon, the Garden was hidden until Truth was found.

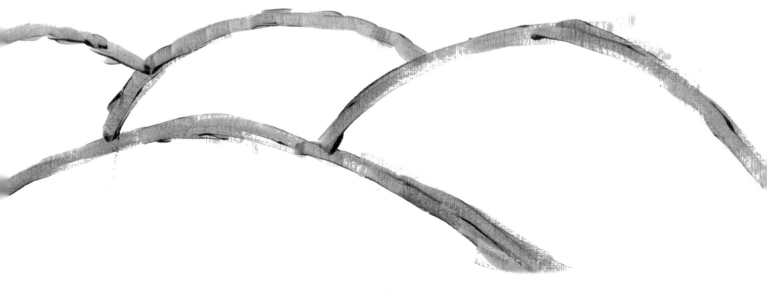

Chapter 7:

The Flood

Darkness was covering the earth again. The Creator searched and finally found an image of Truth. The Creator said, "Life, build an ark so that once again the waters under heaven will be gathered together unto one place." Life built the ark, and it started to rain. The earth was covered with water.

14

Chapter 8:

The Rainbow

Life rode out the storm, and when the water receded, the Creator made a promise: "Life, never again will water cover the earth. As a token of the promise, when a cloud of darkness comes over the earth, I will send a rainbow, the promise of the coming of Light."

Joy

Love

Patience

Chapter 9:

The Journey

The separation between the Creator and Life continued, and the search for Truth grew harder. "Life, where are you? You can start preparing for your return to the Garden. But, first I am sending you on a journey through a land that I will show you." Life replied, "Here I am."

Chapter 10:

Attempt to Destroy Truth

Life started preparing for the journey. This was a threat to the Kingdom of Darkness so Deceit made an attempt to destroy Life once and for all. But again, the Creator found an image of Truth. The image was so small that it had to be hidden.

Chapter 11:

Here I Am

A tiny ark was built out of bulrushes, and the image of Truth was placed therein. The ark was laid by the reeds of the river bank, and once again Life managed to ride out a storm. One day, from out of the midst of a bush, the Creator called to Life, "Life, where are you?" And Life replied, "Here I am."

Chapter 12:

The Wilderness Experience

"Life, I am sending you into the wilderness. A wilderness experience will help you learn how to beware of the wiles of Deceit." All along the way there was a search for Truth, and when found, the Creator would call out.

Chapter 13:

The Call to Truth

"Truth, my eyes run to and fro throughout the whole earth looking for you. When you walk through the water, I will be with you."

"Truth, be strong and of good courage; be not afraid, neither dismayed; for I will be with you wherever I send you."

"Truth, fear not. From the first day that you set your heart to understand, I came to be with you."

"Truth, fear not, you have been chosen for such a time as this."

"Truth, were you there when I laid the foundations of the earth?"

Love

Happiness

4 peace

Chapter 14:

Guilt

Deceit was subtle and always trying to convince Life to make an excuse when an error was made. Life wanted to look good and would make an excuse. Guilt would overshadow Truth, and depression would follow. Life would stumble and lose the Way.

Chapter 15:

Sending Light

Once again, it was becoming very dark on the earth. The Creator called, "Life, where are you?" But Life did not answer. "Life, fear not the darkness. I have a plan. I am sending Light."

Chapter 16:

Life Form of Light

Light arrived on the earth in a life form. Light called out trying to find an image of Truth. "Life, where are you? I am Light. Your rights to the Garden are being restored. The Creator will soon need a gardener." Life whispered, "Here I am."

Chapter 17:

Come, Follow Me

"Life, the Creator has sent me to earth. I am the Rose of Sharon and the Lily of the Valley. I am Truth, and I am the Way back to the Garden and the Tree of Life. Get out of your boat and leave your birth family. Come, follow me."

Chapter 18:

❧

Anger

It made Deceit angry to think that the Creator would send Light to earth in a life form. If the image of Truth started following Light, it would mean the end of the Kingdom of Darkness. The lifeform of Light must be destroyed.

Chapter 19:

Destroyed

Light knew that Deceit was angry so Light spoke to Life. "Life, the Creator loves you very much and sent me in a lifeform as correction for the Garden error. My lifeform will be destroyed, but before it is finished, I will ask the Creator to forgive the error. Then my Light will return to the Creator."

Chapter 20:

Light Speaks

While on earth, Light often spoke to Life. "Life, when the Garden error was made, guilt overshadowed Truth. Truth went missing and caused separation between you and the Creator. The Garden was hidden from view until the error could be corrected and Truth found.

Chapter 21:

Birth Family

To return to the Garden, you must die out to the old self and be born again. You must be pricked in your heart so there can be a rebirth of Truth. Your primary responsibility will no longer be to your birth family but to your heart family. It is a web of Deceit to presume that your birth family is your only family.

Chapter 22:

❧

Heart Family

The heart connection is the real essence and meaning of family. Your heart family is the family you feel at home with. You don't feel a need to belong because you know you belong. Your heart family always seeks Truth.

Chapter 23:

Confession

"After I leave, Deceit will continue to attack. Deceit will always try to use guilt to overshadow Truth. If you make an error, do not hide it. Do not make an excuse and place blame. Confess your error."

Chapter 24:

❦

The Ancient Forest

The earth will become ravaged and appear to be dying. The forests will become ancient before the simplicity of Truth is understood. "Life, where are you? Fear not; a new age of Believers will soon arrive on the earth from many colors, classes, and creeds. They will be willing to spread the gospel of Truth."

Chapter 25:

The New Believer

These new Believers will honor Truth and remain under oath at all times. They will visit the ancient forests. With new found energy and a renewed awareness, they will search for the Light in each lifeform instead of searching for darkness.

Chapter 26:

Forgiveness

Believers will understand that the Garden error was corrected and forgiven. Because they are forgiven, they will forgive themselves and others. They will no longer carry the guilt of the past into the present of today. Guilt will no longer overshadow the Truth of tomorrow.

Chapter 27:

The Awakening

Life was awakened by a rumble of thunder. A blue bird was singing a sweet melody. "Life, where are you? I loved you enough to let you go and trusted you enough to allow you to find your way. Now stay on the path that follows the river. Close your eyes and come join the Light."

Chapter 28:

Welcome Home

The Way is Truth, and Truth is Light. "Life!" "Where are you? Once again it is spring in the Garden. The honeybee has come to drink the sweet nectar. The Whittler has carved your name in the Tree. I am waiting for you with the Rose in the Garden. We're waiting to welcome you Home."

"Life, where are you?"

Life cheerfully answered, "Here I am, Lord. Send me!"

"It is not possible to limit the Creator by our limited minds."

With Love from the Garden,

the Rose

This book was written by my inner child, the Rose. God gave Rose the words for this book, and she believes that if we live our lives with awe and wonder, God will always show us the Way.

Printed in the United States
by Baker & Taylor Publisher Services